Worship Feast

Taizé Songbook

 Abingdon Press

TAIZE SONGBOOK

Worship Feast

09 10 11 12 13—10 9 8 7 6 5 4

Contents

1. Bless the Lord
2. By Night (De noche iremos)
3. Come and Fill (Confitemini Domino)
4. Glory to God (Gloria)
5. In God Alone (Mon âme se repose)
6. In the Lord (El Senyor)
7. Jesus, Remember Me
8. Let Your Servant Now Go in Peace (Nunc Dimittis)
9. Lord Jesus Christ (Jésus le Christ)
10. Nothing Can Trouble (Nada te turbe)
11. O Lord, Hear My Prayer
12. Our Darkness (La ténèbre)
13. Sing Praises (Laudate omnes gentes)
14. Stay With Us (Bleib mit deiner Gnade)
15. Wait for the Lord

Introduction

The songs in this book are so simple, yet so sophisticated and profound. Brother Roger of the Taizé community says that when you sing, you pray twice. These songs are prayers for the heart to sing. Sing them. Memorize them. Let them play in your head and heart all day long. Let God speak deep into your heart through these songs.

Each song has a printed melody line for singers and chords for guitar or keyboard players. Accompanying musicians can listen to the *Worship Feast Taizé* CD (in *Worship Feast Taizé Services: 20 Complete Services in the Spirit of Taizé*) as they practice the songs for your services.

Some of the songs have alternative translations. If you feel comfortable, sing in the other language. Imagine people from around the world gathered around God's throne, singing praises in their own language. That is what the Taizé experience is like.

May all who sing these songs grow more and more in love with God.

Special thanks to the Taizé community and GIA Publications for allowing us to put together this songbook for use with *Worship Feast Taizé Services: 20 Complete Services in the Spirit of Taizé.*

1. Bless the Lord

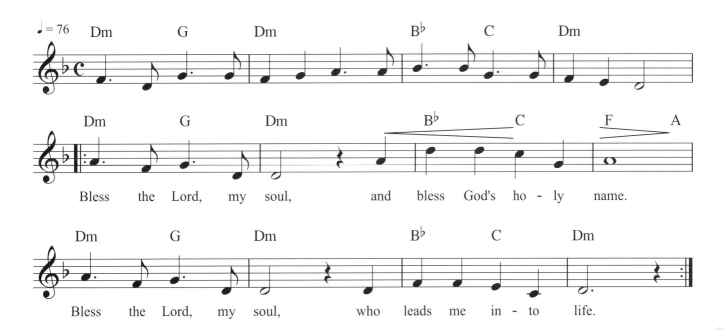

Bless the Lord, my soul, and bless God's ho-ly name.

Bless the Lord, my soul, who leads me in-to life.

MUSIC: Jacques Berthier and the Taizé Community
© 1984 Les Presses de Taizé (France), admin. by GIA Publications, Inc.

Worship Feast: Taizé Songbook

2. By Night
(De noche iremos)

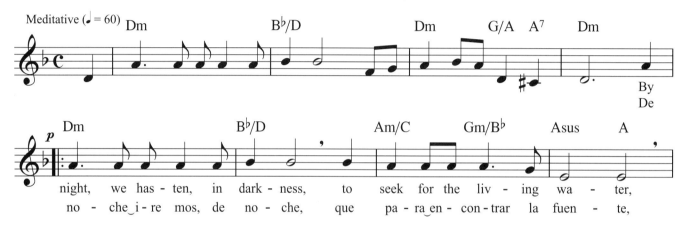

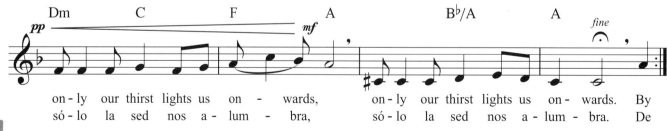

MUSIC: Jacques Berthier

Worship Feast: Taizé Songbook

3. Come and Fill

(Confitemini Domino)

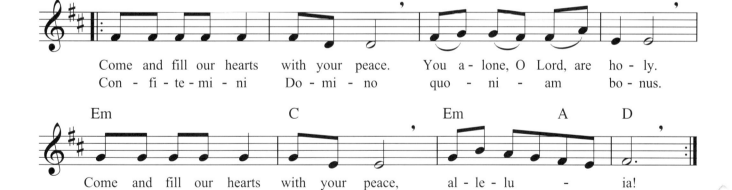

Come and fill our hearts   with your peace.   You a - lone, O Lord, are ho - ly.
Con - fi - te - mi - ni   Do - mi - no   quo - ni - am   bo - nus.

Come and fill our hearts   with your peace,   al - le - lu - - ia!
Con - fi - te - mi - ni   Do - mi - no,   al - le - lu - - ia!

MUSIC: Jacques Berthier
© 1991 Les Presses de Taizé (France), admin. by GIA Publications, Inc.

Worship Feast: Taizé Songbook

4. Glory to God
(Gloria)

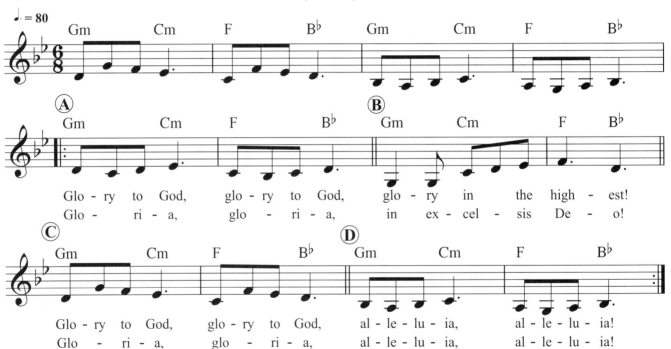

MUSIC: Jacques Berthier
© 1991 Les Presses de Taizé (France), admin. by GIA Publications, Inc.

Worship Feast: Taizé Songbook

5. In God Alone

(Mon âme se repose)

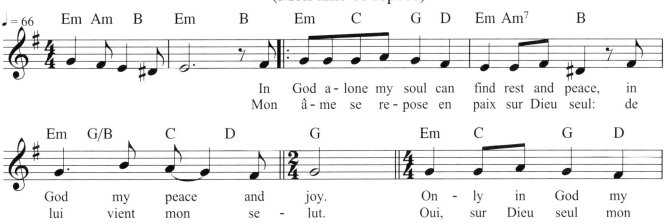

In God a-lone my soul can find rest and peace, in
Mon â-me se re-pose en paix sur Dieu seul: de

God my peace and joy. On - ly in God my
lui vient mon se - lut. Oui, sur Dieu seul mon

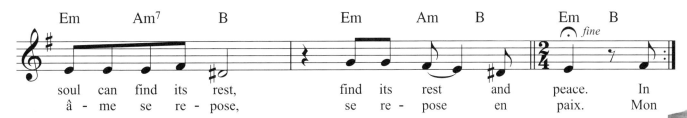

soul can find its rest, find its rest and peace. In
â - me se re - pose, se re - pose en paix. Mon

MUSIC: Jacques Berthier

Worship Feast: Taizé Songbook

6. In the Lord

(El Senyor)

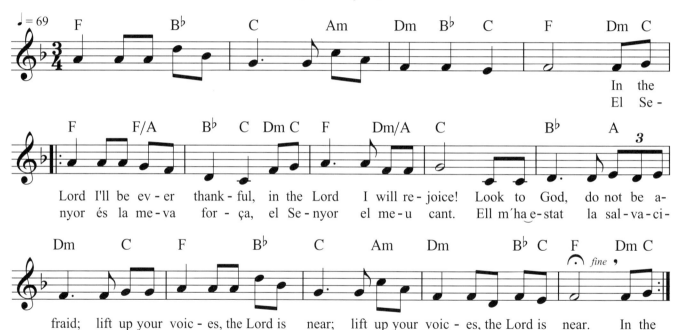

Lyrics beneath the music:

In the
El Se -

Lord I'll be ev - er thank - ful, in the Lord I will re - joice! Look to God, do not be a -
nyor és la me - va for - ça, el Se - nyor el me - u cant. Ell m'ha e - stat la sal - va - ci -

fraid; lift up your voic - es, the Lord is near; lift up your voic - es, the Lord is near. In the
ó. En ell con - fi - o, i no tinc por. En ell con - fi - o, i no tinc por. El Se -

MUSIC: Jacques Berthier

Worship Feast: Taizé Songbook

7. Jesus, Remember Me

Je - sus, re - mem - ber me when you come in - to your king - dom.

Je - sus, re - mem - ber me when you come in - to your king - dom.

MUSIC: Jacques Berthier

Worship Feast: Taizé Songbook

8. Let Your Servant Now Go in Peace

(Nunc Dimittis)

Let your
Nunc di -

ser - vant now go in peace, O Lord,_____ now
mit - tis ser - vum tu - um Do - mi - ne,_____ se -

go in peace ac - cord - ing to your word_____ Let your
cun - dum ver - bum tu - um in pa - ce,_____ Nunc di -

MUSIC: Jacques Berthier

Worship Feast: Taizé Songbook

9. Lord Jesus Christ

(Jésus le Christ)

Lord Je - sus Christ, your light shines with - in us. Let not my doubts nor my dark - ness speak to me.
Jé - sus le Christ, lu - mière in - té - rieu - re, ne lais - se pas mes té - nè - bres me par - ler.

Lord Je - sus Christ, your light shines with - in us. Let my heart al - ways wel - come your love.
Jé - sus le Christ, lu - mière in - té - rieu - re, don - ne - moi d'ac - cueil - lir ton a - mour.

MUSIC: Jacques Berthier
© 1998 Les Presses de Taizé (France), admin. by GIA Publications, Inc.

Worship Feast: Taizé Songbook

10. Nothing Can Trouble
(Nada te turbe)

Noth - ing can trou - ble, noth - ing can fright - en. Those who seek God shall
Na - da te tur - be, na - da te es pan - te. Quien a Dios tie - ne

nev - er go want - ing. God a - lone fills us.
na - da le fal - ta. So - lo Dios bas - ta.

MUSIC: Jacques Berthier
© 1991 Les Presses de Taizé (France), admin. by GIA Publications, Inc.

Worship Feast: Taizé Songbook

11. O Lord, Hear My Prayer

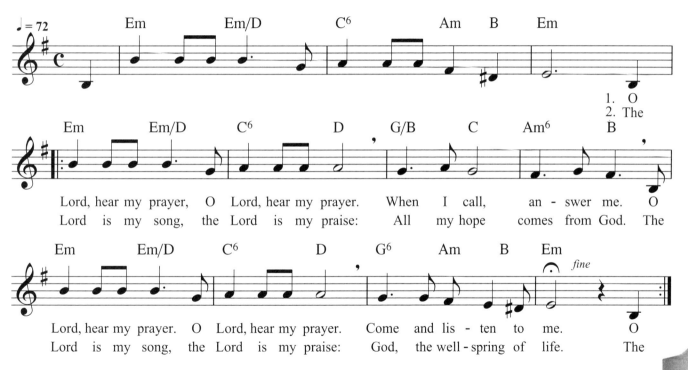

Lord, hear my prayer, O Lord, hear my prayer. When I call, an-swer me. O
Lord is my song, the Lord is my praise: All my hope comes from God. The

Lord, hear my prayer. O Lord, hear my prayer. Come and lis-ten to me. O
Lord is my song, the Lord is my praise: God, the well-spring of life. The

MUSIC: Jacques Berthier
© 1991 Les Presses de Taizé (France), admin. by GIA Publications, Inc.

Worship Feast: Taizé Songbook

12. Our Darkness

(La ténèbre)

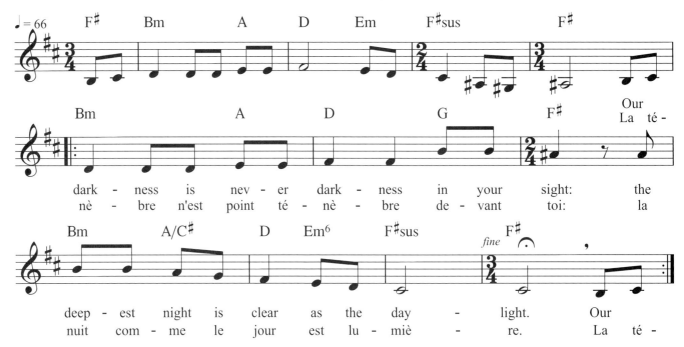

darkness is never darkness in your sight: the
nè - bre n'est point té - nè - bre de - vant toi: la

deep - est night is clear as the day - light. Our
nuit com - me le jour est lu - miè - re. La té -

La té -

MUSIC: Jacques Berthier

Worship Feast: Taizé Songbook

13. Sing Praises

(Laudate omnes gentes)

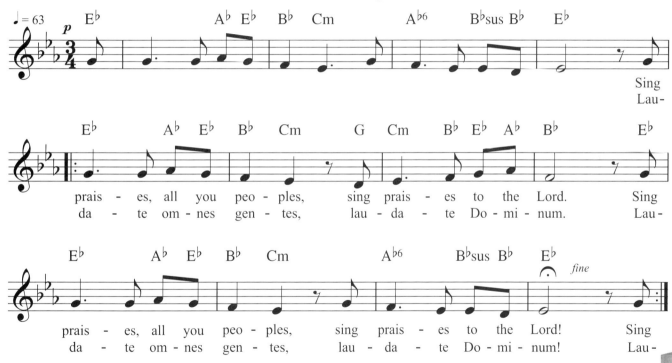

Sing
Lau-

prais - es, all you peo - ples, sing prais - es to the Lord. Sing
da - te om - nes gen - tes, lau - da - te Do - mi - num. Lau-

prais - es, all you peo - ples, sing prais - es to the Lord! Sing
da - te om - nes gen - tes, lau - da - te Do - mi - num! Lau-

MUSIC: Jacques Berthier
© 1991 Les Presses de Taizé (France), admin. by GIA Publications, Inc.

Worship Feast: Taizé Songbook

14. Stay With Us

(Bleib mit deiner Gnade)

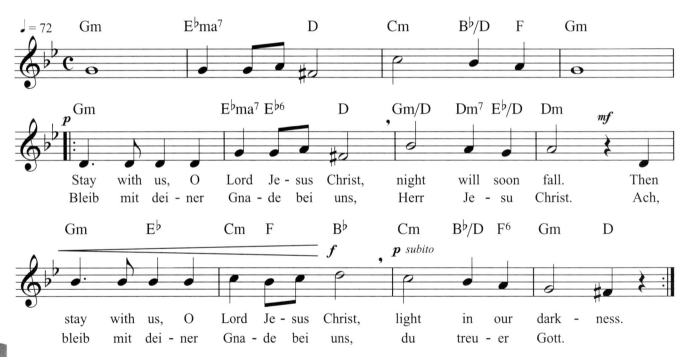

Stay with us, O Lord Je-sus Christ, night will soon fall. Then
Bleib mit dei-ner Gna-de bei uns, Herr Je-su Christ. Ach,

stay with us, O Lord Je-sus Christ, light in our dark-ness.
bleib mit dei-ner Gna-de bei uns, du treu-er Gott.

MUSIC: Jacques Berthier

Worship Feast: Taizé Songbook

15. Wait for the Lord

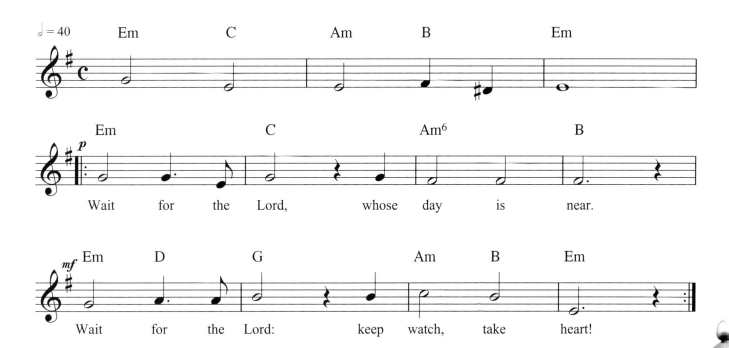

Wait for the Lord, whose day is near.

Wait for the Lord: keep watch, take heart!

MUSIC: Jacques Berthier
© 1998 Les Presses de Taizé (France), admin. by GIA Publications, Inc.

Worship Feast: Taizé Songbook

Youth on their way to prayers in Taizé

A church in the area of Taizé, France

Tory, Peter, 147, 158
Townson, Mike, 181
Trafalgar House, 147–8
Tregear, James, 118–21
Trelford, Donald, 156–8
Troubridge, Tom, 181
'True Stories', 20
Tryon, Dale, 175
Turf Club, 143
TV-am, 144
Twain, Mark, 101
Tweedie, Jill, 135, 181
Tynan, Kenneth, 9, 178

UK Press Gazette, 88
Ulster, 94
Universe, 159
United States of America, 23

Venice, 43, 76
Vestey, Lord, 182
Victoria, Queen, 25–6
Vietnam, 85, 117
Vine, Brian, 133

Wallace, Anna, 182
Wallingford, 23
Wapping, 96
Ward, Christopher, 176
Ward, Richard Somerset, 44
Warhol, Andy, 169
Waterhouse, Keith, 97
Watkins, Alan, 111, 112, 182
Watts, Dennis, 181
Waugh, Auberon, 13, 18, 42, 59,
  112, 117–18, 131, 133, 134, 142,
  143, 149–50, 162, 174; campaign
  against Anthony Shrimsley,
  115–16; Claire Tomalin hoax, 70–
  1; and Dempster, 67–8; *Diaries*,
  72; and the Jeremy Thorpe case,
  25, 130; Nora Beloff case, 48, 72–
  3; opposition to Hislop, 33, 37–9,
  41; relations with Ingrams, 31–2,
  54–5, 69, 75–7; resignation, 31–3,
  46, 77–8; techniques, 72–5

Waugh, Evelyn, 32, 69, 168
Waugh, Margaret, 32
Webster, Martin, 182
Weidenfeld, Lord, 178–9
Wells, John, 21, 81, 89, 90–2, 138,
  177, 182
Wesker, Arnold, 182
West, Richard, 13, 38, 43, 85–6, 90,
  112, 117
Western Daily Press, 55
Wheatcroft, Geoffrey, 19, 41, 179, 182
White, Sam, 107
White's Club, 144
Whitehall Theatre, London, 91
Whitelaw, William, 178
Who's Who, 29, 57–62, 86–7, 89, 135
Wien, Judge, 106, 139
Wilcox, Desmond, 135, 170
Wilcox, Patsy, 135
Williams, Shirley, 180
Wilson, A. N., 19
Wilson, Charlie, 173
Wilson, Harold, 9, 79, 101, 107,
  108, 110, 126–8, 130, 131, 138,
  151, 152, 172, 183
Wilson, Mary, 126, 138
The Windsor Letters, 20
Winn, Godfrey, 183
Wintour, Anna, 28
Wintour, Charles, 28–9, 172, 174,
  177
Witchell, Nicholas, 178
Wodehouse, P. G., 75, 164–5
Wogan, Terry, 7, 52
Wontner, Sir Hugh, 183
Woodhouse, Adrian, 170
'The World Of Books', 19–20
Worsthorne, Peregrine, 73, 75, 183
Wyatt, Woodrow, 183

Yentob, Alan, 168
York, Peter, 52
Yorkshire Ripper, 136
You magazine, 41

Zorza, Victor, 183

Sands, Bobby, 15
Sandys, Duncan, 172
Sassie, Victor, 22
Saudi Arabia, 95
Savoy Hotel, London, 126
Scargill, Arthur, 164, 179
Schulman, Milton, 179–80
Scott, Norman, 130
Scruton, Dr Roger, 179
Sedgemore, Brian, 150
Sellers, Peter, 179
Servadio, Gaia, 177
Shah, Eddy, 21–2
Shah of Persia, 180
Shrewsbury school, 12
Shrimsley, Anthony, 115–16, 134,
  181
Shrimsley, Bernard, 115–16, 134,
  180
Silvester, Christopher, 17–18, 21,
  27, 32, 33–4, 40, 42, 59–60, 88–9,
  90
Silvester, Victor, 17
Skinner, Judge, 71
'Slagheap Affair', 127
Slater, James, 103, 104
Slater Walker, 103
Slaughter, Audrey, 172
'Slicker' *see* Gillard, Michael
Smith, Helen, 95
Smith, T. Dan, 104
Smith, W. H., 46, 162, 180
Snow, C. P., 180
Soames, Emma, 178
Soames, Lord, 169, 178, 180
Soames, Nicholas, 169
Socialist Worker, 96
Socialist Worker's Party, 93
Sounds, 53
South Africa, 130
Soviet Union, 127, 128
'Spanker' case, 44
The Spectator, 29, 31, 51, 54–5, 72,
  75, 85, 90, 117, 133, 141, 157
'Spitting Image', 14, 53–4, 159
The Sporting Life, 84

Stalker, John, 94
Stamp, Gavin, 19
Standard, 19, 37, 40, 41, 96, 122; *see
  also Evening Standard*
Star, 147, 148, 158
Stassinopoulos, Arianna, 90, 173
Status magazine, 59
Steel, David, 150–1, 169
Sternberg, Rudy, 127
Stevens, Jocelyn, 134, 146, 178
Steven, Stewart, 62–3, 151–2, 180
Stonehouse, John, 138
Streep, Meryl, 181
'Street of Shame' column, 37, 47,
  109, 181
Strong, Dr Roy, 180
Sun, 52
Sunday Express, 87, 126, 144, 145–7
Sunday Mirror, 47–8, 60
Sunday Telegraph, 31, 75, 114, 160
Sunday Times, 16, 23, 34, 35–6, 40,
  65, 66, 67, 70–2, 99, 101, 111–12,
  114, 180–1
Sunday Today, 90
Switzerland, 141

Tatler, 112, 113
Taylor, A. J. P., 43, 76
Taylor, Teddy, 17
Tebbit, Norman, 169–70, 177
Tennant, Emma, 89–90
Terry, Walter, 127
That Was The Week That Was, 92
Thatcher, Denis, 91–2, 132
Thatcher, Margaret, 53, 63, 64,
  91–2, 94, 110, 111, 143, 146, 149
  159, 162, 168
Theodoracopoulos, Taki, 28, 144
Thornton, Michael, 20
Thorpe, Jeremy, 25, 70, 114, 129–31
Thorpe, Marion, 129
The Times, 48–9, 75, 111, 113,
  114–15, 116–18, 141
Today, 21–2
Tomalin, Claire, 70–1, 78
Tomkinson, Martin, 82–4, 86